YOUR KNOWLEDGE HAS VALUE

AF143546

Bibliographic information published by the German National Library:

The German National Library lists this publication in the National Bibliography; detailed bibliographic data are available on the Internet at http://dnb.dnb.de .

Imprint:

Copyright © 2016 GRIN Verlag, Open Publishing GmbH
Print and binding: Books on Demand GmbH, Norderstedt Germany
ISBN: 9783668304246

This book at GRIN:

http://www.grin.com/en/e-book/340929/september-11-2001-political-consequences

Florian Wolf

September 11, 2001. Political consequences

GRIN Publishing

GRIN - Your knowledge has value

Since its foundation in 1998, GRIN has specialized in publishing academic texts by students, college teachers and other academics as e-book and printed book. The website www.grin.com is an ideal platform for presenting term papers, final papers, scientific essays, dissertations and specialist books.

Visit us on the internet:

http://www.grin.com/

http://www.facebook.com/grincom

http://www.twitter.com/grin_com

September 11, 2001 – Political consequences

Florian Wolf

Stufe K1

Schuljahr
2015/2016

Fach: Englisch

Gymnasium am Romäusring

"One of the worst days in America's history saw some of the bravest acts in Americans' history. We'll always honor the heroes of 9/11. And here at this hallowed place, we pledge that we will never forget their sacrifice."[1]

—President George W. Bush at the Pentagon in 2008

---

[1] http://communitytable.parade.com/125076/compiledandeditedbysaralukinson/09-tribute-to-9-11/

Table of contents

1 General information

1.1 Founding and development of al-Qaeda

The father of Osama bin Laden, Mohammed bin Laden, was the founder of an Arabic building company. He founded this company in 1931, back then he already had good connections to the royal family in Saudi Arabia. Mohammed gained a lot of power with his building company and he was a prestigious businessman. He founded several daughter companies. With this wealth, his power and the good relationships to the royal family he had a lot of influence in Saudi Arabia. [2]

In the 1950s Saudi Arabia got extremely rich because of the oil and the average income of a Saudi was bigger than the average income of an American. This led into a split of the society. There was a small group of people who were very rich and a lot of people who were extremely poor. Before then Saudi Arabia was underdeveloped and in a minimum of time there were televisions, streets and schools. The majority of the people were until then nomads and they became disoriented and started to reject the changes. These nomads searched for help and found it in their faith to deal with those innovations. This movement to their faith was like a foundation of the radicalization and anti-American attitude because the Americans brought those innovations into their perception. [3]

Osama bin Laden was born on March 10, 1957 and was one of the 77 children of his father Mohammed bin Laden. In 1957, when his father was already, a billionaire he had overall 22 wives. [4] Early on Osama orientated oneself towards an extreme direction of his faith. He was pious, diligent and disciplined. The faith gave him help and affection. [5]

The People's Democratic Party of Afghanistan (PDPA) assumed power with a military coup in 1978 and the majority of the population started to reject this government. The PDPA had a lot of enemies in their own country when the civil war started in 1979. The government needed the help of the Soviet Union and the civil war escalated.

---

[2] Der Tod wird euch finden 2007, p. 82
[3] Der Tod wird euch finden 2007, p. 110 et seq.
[4] https://en.wikipedia.org/wiki/Mohammed_bin_Awad_bin_Laden#Wives_and_children (08.02.2016)
[5] Der Tod wird euch finden 2007, p. 91

The Soviet Union wanted to bring peace and to substitute the government with a Moscow-friendly government. The mission ended in an invasion. [6]

Osama bin Laden started to fight against the Soviets and he wanted to fight with some other Arabs to continue the holy war in other countries. He wanted to defend and to promote the Islam. These Arabs were so called Mujahideen. [7]

In August 1988 Osama bin Laden founded al-Qaeda with an ideological foundation. In the second Gulf War (1990/1991) they radicalized and formed an anti-American opposition. They were angry due to the non-attendance of Muslim troops on the Saudi Arabian territory and the commitment of American troops in Arabic states. [8]

Egyptian subgroups started to plan the overthrow of their royal family in Egypt. With the support of the USA it was not possible to overthrow the royal family and al-Qaeda started to hate the USA more and more. The subgroups had to leave Egypt and they started to reinforce their power in Afghanistan. This reinforcement was benefited by the ascent of the Taliban in Afghanistan. In 1996 al-Qaeda declared war against the USA. From 1998 al-Qaeda gained more and more recruits from North Africa. [9] Instead of being a huge group al-Qaeda always consisted of several subgroups with different and equal intentions. In 1998 al-Qaeda started to plan the attacks on the September 11, 2001. Osama bin Laden was from 1999 on public enemy number one of the USA and his head money amounted to 25 Mio. US-Dollars. [10]

Osama bin Laden was killed on May 1, 2011 by Navy Seals and Ayman az-Zawahiri replaced him as the commander.

Al-Qaeda needs a lot of money for vehicles, weapons, explosive, communication, recruitment, propaganda and livelihood for their members. They are gaining this money by kidnapping foreign citizens to get ransom money. [11] The heritage from Mohammed bin Laden is quite important too. They are also dealing with drugs like opium, diamonds from Africa and weapons. [12] There are speculations that the royal

---

[6] https://en.wikipedia.org/wiki/War_in_Afghanistan_(1978–present) (08.02.2016)
[7] https://en.wikipedia.org/wiki/Mujahideen#Afghanistan (08.02.2016)
[8] http://www.bpb.de/politik/extremismus/islamismus/36374/al-qaida?p=all (08.02.2016)
[9] http://www.bpb.de/politik/extremismus/islamismus/36374/al-qaida?p=all (08.02.2016)
[10] Der heilige Krieg 2011, p. 304
[11] http://www.sueddeutsche.de/politik/westliche-geiseln-eu-laender-finanzieren-al-qaida-mit-millionen-loesegeldern-1.2069656 (21.01.2016)
[12] http://www.wiwo.de/politik/ausland/al-qaida-dem-geld-der-terroristen-auf-der-spur-seite-3/4637972-3.html (21.01.2016)

family of Saudi Arabian is one of the main sponsors.[13] Splitting Al-Qaeda in several subgroups is an important advantage because it is easier to hide money transfers and money laundering through offshore accounts and charity organizations.

1.2 Ideology and aims

The main intention of al-Qaeda is the representation of the Islam towards anti-Islam acting countries. They think that there is a complot of the USA, Israel and Europe against the Islam and they want to fight against that.[14] Al-Qaeda legitimates their acting with the Koran, especially with its original form so they have to fight against infidels. The modern western world is representing in their eyes an irreligious, unbridled and socialistic society and in their opinion they have to conduct war against socialism and atheism.[15]

Al-Qaedas first attacks were already in the 1990s but they only kill enemies and no civilians at least in their opinion. They are using those acts of violence for propaganda in their own countries to recruit new members. The main war location is the Iraq.

With its economical and political dominance the West is representing the main enemy and al-Qaeda wants to release all Arabic countries from the western influence. They want to prevent the spread of western goods and the western lifestyle. In the opinion of the al-Qaeda supporters especially the USA is representing these changes. Their tactic includes the strengthening of their own network and the infiltration of their enemies like the USA.

In addition, we can say that al-Qaeda turns against emancipation of women, the consumption of alcohol, homosexuality, nudity and sex out of wedlock.[16]

1.3 Planning of the attacks

Al-Qaeda has recruiters all over the world especially in important metropolises. Either the recruiters are Arabic and they entered the country or they already live in this

---

[13] http://www.spiegel.de/politik/ausland/saudi-arabien-al-qaida-angeblich-vom-koenigshaus-finanziert-a-1016612.html (21.01.2016)
[14] http://news.bbc.co.uk/2/shared/spl/hi/pop_ups/04/world_al_qaeda/html/2.stm (08.02.2016)
[15] http://www.infoplease.com/spot/al-qaeda-terrorism.html (08.02.2016)
[16] https://en.wikipedia.org/wiki/Al-Qaeda (08.02.2016)

country and then convert to the extremism. For example at universities al-Qaeda is searching for new members for their fight against the West and to collect information about possible targets. Al-Qaeda started in 1999 the planning of the attacks in September 11, 2001. 15 of the 19 assassins were Saudis. All assassins were all from wealthy, respected, worldly and less religious families. [17] The assassins were well educated and some of them had the possibility to make a semester abroad. While the students were abroad they started to contact radical preachers and identified oneself with their ideology and aims. That is the main reasons why they decided to become martyrs. Four of them studied at the German university in Hamburg and they contacted al-Qaeda. All assassins were in constant touch with Osama bin Laden. To get educated they flew to Afghanistan and al-Qaeda prepared them for the attacks. Three of the four German students and another student who studied in the USA started to take flight hours and some of them gained a license to fly.[18] Concerning the beginning of planning the attacks, the resources are quite conflicting. Some resources report that the planning took more than ten years but they agree with each other that al-Qaeda was in contact with willing martyrs since 1999.

2   The Attack

2.1 Short overview about the events

The hijackers took control of four commercial airlines in the early morning of September 11, 2001. They hijacked two Boeing 757s and two Boeing 767s.
The goals of the hijackers were the World Trade Center towers, the Pentagon and the White House.
The four flights were:

- American Airlines Flight 11 (AA 11, red route):
  At 8:14 a.m. five assassins hijacked the Boeing 767 that flew from Boston to Los Angeles. At 8:46 a.m. the plane hit the North Tower of the World Trade Center. At this time the people still though that this was an accident. The North Tower collapsed at 10:28 a.m..
- United Airlines Flight 175 (UA 175, dark red route):

---

[17] https://en.wikipedia.org/wiki/September_11_attacks#Planning_of_the_attacks (08.02.2016)
[18] http://voices.nationalgeographic.com/2011/09/07/the-original-plans-for-911/ (08.02.2016)

The Boeing 767 got hijacked by five men between 8:42 a.m. and 8:46 a.m.. At 9:03 a.m. they flew the plane into the South Tower of the World Trade Center which finally collapsed at 9:59 a.m..

- American Airlines flight 77 (AA 77, green route):
  The Boeing 757 flew from Virginia to Los Angeles and got hijacked at 8:51 a.m. by five men. The plane hit the Pentagon at 9:37 a.m..

- United Airlines Flight 93 (UA 93, blue route):
  The four hijackers took control over the Boeing 757 at 9:28 a.m. and changed its route. Passengers tried to overcome the hijackers and the airplane crashed at 10:03 a.m. into the ground near Shanksville, Pennsylvania.

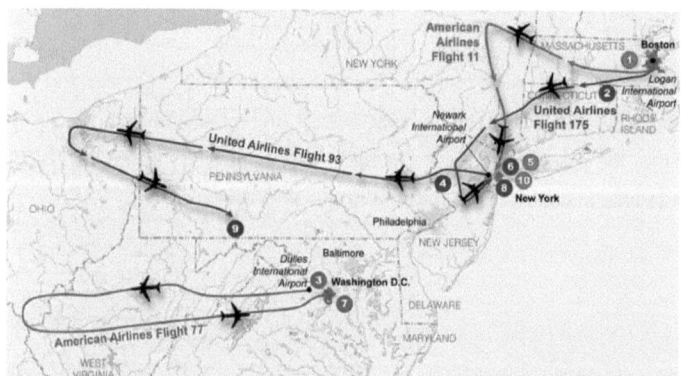

Image 1

About 3000 people died at September 11, 2001 and more than 15.000 people could escape from the World Trade Center to save their lives. At November 1, 2004 Osama bin Laden published a video in which he admits that al-Qaeda planned these attacks and he names reasons for the attacks. He threats with more attacks, if the US-government won't stop supporting Israel.

2.2 First reactions of several institutions

President George W. Bush said, "America was targeted for attack because we're the brightest beacon for freedom and opportunity in the world."[19] He also added that this were attacks against the "American way of life" [20] and against the American

---

[19] http://edition.cnn.com/2001/US/09/11/bush.speech.text/ (09.02.2016)
[20] http://edition.cnn.com/2001/US/09/11/bush.speech.text/ (09.02.2016)

"Freedom".[21]Millions of American citizens demonstrated to show and reinforce their patriotism and their condolence. The anger against Arabic and Muslim mounted and nowadays there is still a gap and not 100% trust. On September 11, 2001 it was the first time that the NATO was triggering the case for the alliance and they pledged unfettered solidarity. Many countries supported the USA in their "fight against the terror"[22] as Bush called it and the countries had the choice between being "either with us [the USA] or against us [the USA]".[23] Supporters were for example Germany, Australia and the United Kingdom.

The European Union had gone through several changes after September 11 concerning their safety of the states. They wanted to intensify their cooperation with the American anti-terror authorities and also their efforts against terror financing.[24] Especially the air-safety got improved and they developed international legislatives instruments to optimize the fight against terrorists.[25]

Gerhard Schroeder commented that the attacks were "not only attacks on the people in the United States, our friends in America, but also against the entire civilized world, against our own freedom, against our own values, values which we share with the American people. We will not let these values be destroyed."[26]

3 Political consequences

3.1 New laws – USA Patriot Act

The Twin Towers were a symbol of the financial markets so the attacks were also against the economy and the capitalism. The Pentagon is representing the military power. Both places weren't defendable although they are showing the strength and power of America. The attacks of September 11th were against the only superpower and they were in a period of peace. That is the reason why America is unsettled and has to react. One of Bush's solutions was the USA PATRIOT Act. Patriot Act stands for Uniting and Strengthening America by Providing Appropriate Tools Required to

---

[21] http://edition.cnn.com/2001/US/09/11/bush.speech.text/ (09.02.2016)
[22] http://edition.cnn.com/2001/US/11/06/gen.attack.on.terror/ (09.02.2016)
[23] http://edition.cnn.com/2001/US/11/06/gen.attack.on.terror/ (09.02.2016)
[24] Keine Macht dem Terror 2001, p. 217 et seq.
[25] Keine Macht dem Terror 2001, p. 128; 131
[26] http://www.history.com/topics/reaction-to-9-11 (03.01.2016)

Intercept and Obstruct Terrorism Act. The Patriot Act is given several intelligences more discretionary to develop and implement anti-terror methods. Law-barrages, which restricted the anti-terror methods, are now abrogated. The main intention was the prevention of other terroristic attacks and the financing of terrorist activities.[27]

The Patriot Act contains ten titles with various contents.

CIA, FBI and the NSA are now allowed to intercept telephone conversations and internet-communication without a judge as a supervisory authority. They have to inform the judge, but he has to agree. The spying possibilities were extremely extended and the intelligence agencies are more powerful. Another important aspect is that the intelligence agencies are now allowed to execute a search warrant without informing the regarding person.[28] Telephone companies and Internet service providers have to provide the data of their users to the agencies without being allowed to tell the users. This data contains for example your phone calls or telephone conferences, information about your locations or your text messages. This is against the privacy of the citizens! The FBI now has because of the Patriot Act the access to all banking information even if they have no evidence for a crime. This is also against the privacy of the citizens. The CIA is now also allowed to investigate inside the USA. Before the Patriot Act was released the CIA was only allowed to ascertain outside the USA.

The border-security got also extremely "improved" because the authorities are now allowed to retain immigrants without naming reason for an unlimited of time (the maximum is 6 months) and to deport them, also without mentioning reasons.[29] The electrical systems at the borders were also quite upgraded. The authorities have now the possibilities of face- and car registration number detection, to immediately catch criminals. Regarding the privacy this is quite concerning as well, but in the USA nearly everything is allowed to save the state and the citizens. This is also firmly established in the mentality of a huge part of the population.

The exchange of information between the different agencies got also improved by establishing a common database with all information that has ever been collected. To travel round the USA you now need a PNR (passenger name record) with personal information about your journey like: the duration of your journey, your address with

---

[27] https://www.opensocietyfoundations.org/events/usa-patriot-acts-effect-civil-liberties (07.02.2016)
[28] http://www.dw.com/de/usa-patriot-act-das-neue-anti-terror-paket/a-351266 (07.02.2016)
[29] http://www.taz.de/!5080880/ (07.02.2016)

telephone numbers and your mail address and whereabouts like your booked hotel/apartment.[30][31] This information is saved on servers for several weeks even after your journey. Several of those titles are violating the right of for example the privacy or the data privacy. Most of the times the agencies do not need reasons to get for instance banking information and the judge has to agree, if there is a judge at all. If they need to name reasons, it is more than enough, if there is a terror suspicion.

This is one of the main problems with the Patriot Act. Firstly it is not allowed to intercept people or the population without reasons and without a legal base. Secondly it is not allowed to save so many data about people without letting them know and thirdly the terror suspicion is quite vulnerable for an abuse, because the defense department defines what a "terror suspicion" is.[32] Law is not equal to the moral and nearly everything is allowed to save the lives of the citizens and the national security.

Another important point of criticism is that the Patriot Act was originally determined to fight against the terror but it is nowadays more and more used to fight against normal crime and drug cartels. That is the reason why more and more innocent people are getting intercepted.

The Patriot Act also forces foreign daughter companies of American companies to reveal data about their users and this is in the European Union for example prohibited. Many people are concerned about their data and European companies are worried, that this information will be used for industrial espionage.

One of the main principles of the USA is the system of checks and balances. The Patriot Act is explicit prohibiting supervisory authorities and is ruining this principle.[33]

Due to the Patriot Act intelligence agencies had nearly unrestricted radius of operation since 2001. 2015 some parts of the Patriot Act expired and did not get extended immediately because the citizens were afraid of the espionage without a legal base.[34] There was also a formation of a lobby because IT-companies wanted to tell their users about the requests from the agencies and they were afraid of loosing the users trust. Some senators were also against an extension because they wanted

---

[30] https://en.wikipedia.org/wiki/Passenger_name_record (09.02.2016)
[31] http://searchdatamanagement.techtarget.com/definition/Patriot-Act (07.02.2016)
[32] http://pretioso-blog.com/was-man-ueber-den-usa-patriot-act-wissen-sollte/#.Vrn--MdK1uV (07.02.2016)
[33] http://www.dw.com/de/usa-patriot-act-das-neue-anti-terror-paket/a-351266 (07.02.2016)
[34] http://www.zeit.de/politik/2015-06/us-senat-patriot-acts (09.02.2016)

to get votes. In contrast to all these facts, the expired parts got substituted by the USA FREEDOM Act, which includes nearly the same.[35] Although the Patriot Act is not completely comfortable with the law it is still the most important instrument in the war against the terror (and normal crimes). Espionage is in the USA way more tolerated and legitimized. Another reason why the Patriot Act is so tolerated in the USA is the fact that you might seem "unpatriotic" if you dislike it and many people in the USA do not understand how extensive the espionage is or they even do not want to know it.[36]

3.2 Monitoring by the NSA

The September 11, 2001 was extremely bitter for the intelligence agencies. They intercepted several conversations between the hijackers but they failed. The conversations were saved but not translated until November 12, 2001. After these failures the confidence of the agencies decreased. George W. Bush and his vice president Dick Cheney wanted to take revenge on the Iraq although the National Security Agency (NSA) knew that the attacks were from al-Qaeda and the Iraq was innocent.[37] An extension of the security services was a direct follow of September 11, 2001. They needed more rights and more staff and the legal situation was completely indifferent.

Since George W. Bush signed the Patriot Act, the NSA can nearly do everything without getting controlled. Since then the analyst of the NSA are working 24 hours per day and seven days a week. The NSA is getting "controlled" by the so-called Foreign Intelligence Surveillance Act (FISA) and from so-called FISA-courts. This law should prevent misusages and infringements of the forth amendment. [38] This amendment does not allow for example the confiscation without an affidavit. The FISA courts are also "controlling" the activities of the NSA for example. To circumvent the law and the courts the government invented a special legal position for metadata. Metadata are information about who called who, when from where and

---

[35] https://www.rt.com/usa/264005-freedom-patriot-act-surveillance/ (09.02.2016)
[36] http://www.faz.net/aktuell/politik/ausland/antiterrorgesetze-patriot-act-gilt-weiter-1637729.html (07.02.2016)
[37] Der NSA-Komplex 2015, p. 111 et seq.
[38] https://en.wikipedia.org/wiki/Foreign_Intelligence_Surveillance_Act (10.02.2016)

how long. For this information the NSA does not need a judge to agree and it is extremely easy to get the actual content of the phone call with these metadata.

Nowadays the attacks of September 11, 2001 are an important argument to get more and more money (several hundreds billions of dollars budget per year, for their staff, servers and buildings)[39] from the Congress for the intelligence agencies, especially for the NSA.[40]

The September 11, 2001 was for the intelligence agencies an really important day. To protect the USA more and more companies wanted to help the agencies and they were willing to cooperate with them. Particularly Internet service providers and telecommunication companies are important for the espionage of America and not American calls and internet activities. That cooperation allowed the NSA to intercept nearly 81% of all in- and out coming calls of the USA in October 8, 2001.[41]

Another important and characteristic aspect for the USA is the privatization of the espionage. These companies are so called technological advisers" but they are doing exactly the same as the governmental authorities. The privatization costs the government yearly several hundred millions of dollars.[42] One of the most important partners is a company called "Booz Allen Hamilton". The company has about 24.000 employees and they are offering military services for the Pentagon.[43] Interesting are the avails before and after September 11, 2001. Before September 11, 2001 the company had an avail of nearly 330 millions of dollars per year and ten years after September 11, 2001 the avail increased up to more than 3,3 billions of dollars per year and roughly 99% of its orders are coming from the Pentagon. In 2015 the company had an avail of more than 5,8 billions of dollars per year. They are offering services like maintenances of servers, development of software and espionage.[44]

Another important partner of the NSA is for example the American company Dell. Dell is servicing all servers of the NSA that are located in Japan.

The privatization has a huge advantage for the government. The intelligence agencies are gaining a lot of information without being in touch with the espionage and their breach of the law. Nowadays more than 70% of the "black budget" of the

---

[39] Der NSA-Komplex 2015, p. 115 et seq.
[40] Der NSA-Komplex 2015, p. 115 et seq.
[41] Der NSA-Komplex 2015, p. 139 et seq.
[42] Der NSA-Komplex 2015, p. 47 et seq.
[43] https://en.wikipedia.org/wiki/Booz_Allen_Hamilton (10.02.2016)
[44] Der NSA-Komplex 2015, p. 47 et seq.

agencies is spent on private companies. This is way more expensive than doing it oneself would be.

The borders of a constitutional state are more and more shifted due to the White House and the September 11, 2001. Before the attacks the program Echelon was extremely criticized. It is a program to intercept satellites to get information about telephone calls. After September 11, 2001 the program was unconditional accepted.

One of the most important aspects to gain information is the cooperation with other countries and their intelligence agencies. The NSA is for instance working together with the German Bundesnachrichtendienst

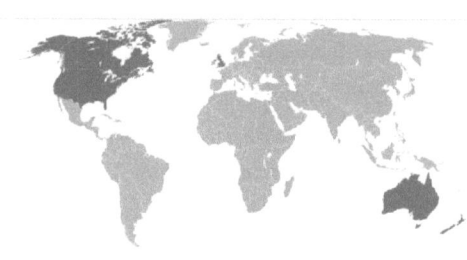
Image 2

(BND), the Israeli agencies and many other western countries. The most important cooperation is so called the Five Eyes. The Five Eyes is an international intelligence alliance comprising the USA, the United Kingdom, Canada, Australia and New Zealand (Image 3).[45]

The NSA has several programs and divisions for specific themes.

The Tempora program was invented by the United Kingdom but they are sharing all information with the NSA. The task of the Tempora program is to get all of the European internet traffic. It does not matter which rights are getting injured they just want all data. To get this information the United Kingdom is tapping the fiber optic cables and every data packet, which is flowing through the United Kingdom, is getting saved. The agency is making "full takes". This means that all data is getting saved for about three to four days but after that time it is not getting completely deleted because the metadata is getting saved forever on the servers of the NSA and the Government Communications Headquarters (GCHQ). The GCHQ is the British NSA. If a particular person is getting targeted from an analyst because he or the program has a suspicion all of the persons data is getting saved forever until he is getting untagged.[46]

---

[45] Der NSA-Kompley 2015, p. 75 et seq.
[46] Der NSA-Komplex 2015, p. 76 et seq.

Through those interfaces the agencies are collecting more than 40 billions of data packets per day.[47] The BND is also involved. The European data is for example getting analyzed from an old Sony factory hall in San Antonio, Texas.[48]

Another important NSA division is the Special Sources Operations department (SSO). This department has a nearly unrestricted budget and they are developing new programs and hardware mechanisms. They are intern called the "Elite of the NSA" and they are gaining more and more information per day. They are responsible for spying other countries like Afghanistan, Jordan or China.[49] They are collecting approximately 75% of all metadata and they developed software techniques to scan the data for keywords so they can find them again with search algorithms. They are also using the hardware of devices for the espionage.[50]

The most important and best known program to spy is called Prism. This program is collecting data from servers in the USA. After September 11, 2001 many companies started to cooperate with the NSA like Microsoft, Google, Apple, Facebook, Skype (Microsoft). With the cooperation of these companies the NSA, especially Prism, is able to have access to the data of their clouds and servers. This gives the NSA so much information about nearly every citizen for example in the USA because nearly everybody has a device from on of these companies. The can take this information directly from their servers and the companies are helping them and they are not allowed to tell their users because of the Patriot Act.[51]

Nowadays the NSA is not only spying in foreign countries, they are also intercepting their own citizens due to the "prevention of September 11, 2001 2.0". Internal documents of the NSA, leaked by one of the most important Whistleblowers Edward Snowden, are telling us, that the NSA does not want to prevent September 11, 2001 2.0, they want the dominance of the internet and of the information because information stands for power. With an budged of more than 10,6 billions of dollars per year, more than 40.000 employees and a new data center in Utah[52] for more than 1,2

---

[47] Der NSA-Komplex 2015, p. 127
[48] Der NSA-Komplex 2015, p. 116 et seq.
[49] Der NSA-Komplex, p. 129 et seq.
[50] Der NSA-Komplex, p. 144 et seq.
[51] Der NSA-Komplex, p. 133 et seq.
[52] http://www.theatlantic.com/technology/archive/2015/11/a-visit-to-the-nsas-data-center-in-utah/416691/ (10.02.2016)

billions of dollars[53] is the NSA more than just a little danger. "That an analyst can target every citizen no matter when", should make us wonder.[54]

3.3 Iraq war

After September 11, 2001 America started to intensify the war against the terror and possible attacks. One of these possibilities was the Iraq. Saddam Hussein was the premier minister of the Iraq since 1999 and he reigned the country dictatorial. The USA said that they have information about mass destruction weapons and they said that the Iraq is posing a threat to the USA and all other countries with those weapons and its connections to al-Qaeda.[55] The goal of the USA was the disempowerment of the premier minister, to setup a democracy in the Iraq and to destroy all of their weapons. They gave Hussein an ultimatum and after that they started to bomb Bagdad. They called this war a preemptive war. Both of their reasons were provable wrong. Several Agents of the United Nations (UN) searched for multiple months in the Iraq for those weapons, but they could not find anything.[56] The other reason, that the Iraq had connections to al-Qaeda, was also a lie because al-Qaeda came after the plunge of Hussein.

The USA did not get a mandate of the UN but attacked the Iraq anyway, which is illegal. They promised to destroy mass destruction weapons, which was a lie. They also promised to catch terrorists and to search for information of terror-networks, which is also a lie. The most important reason why the Iraq War was a failure is that they promised to give humanitarian help, but the opposite happened. Millions of people had to live without water, food and medicine. Instead of helping the Iraq felt into a civil war, the US forces scavenged schools, museums, army depots and ministries. This is an infringement of the Geneva Convention.[57]

---

[53] http://www.handelsblatt.com/technik/it-internet/rechenzentrum-des-geheimdiensts-nsa-platz-fuer-fuenf-billionen-gigabyte/8315424.html (10.02.2016)
[54] Der NSA-Komplex, p. 86
[55] https://www.lpb-bw.de/irak_krieg.html (24.01.2016)
[56] https://en.wikipedia.org/wiki/Rationale_for_the_Iraq_War#Formal_search_after_the_invasio n (09.02.2016)
[57] http://www.zeit.de/2013/12/Irakkrieg-Folgen-Bilanz (24.01.2016)

Instead of helping, the USA might had some other reason to fight in the Iraq. It is expected, that the USA firstly wanted to gain control over the oil reserves.[58] To gain control over those resources, they had to substitute Hussein with an America-friendly regime. Secondly, they wanted a good geological position for the Middle East conflict to support Israel.

Summing up, we can say that the Iraq is after eight years allocation through the USA and five more years still very instable. The status of the Iraq is far apart from a democracy and peace. Nearly monthly there are terrorist attacks in the Iraq and the population is in a bad shape. Nowadays we know that the USA used lies to promote for the Iraq war, they had no UN mandate but they attacked the Iraq anyway. Nevertheless there weren't any consequences for the USA and they are still asserting, that the September 11th had nothing to do with the Iraq War.[59]

4 Current political situation

4.1 Obamas changes

Obamas inauguration was at January 17, 2009. He promoted transparency regarding the governance and especially the espionage affaire. He said that whistleblowers are the most important source for the enlightenment of the American society. In contrast to that five whistleblowers got charged while he was in office, more than as never before. Some of those whistleblowers even got the death penalty and some of them will spend their lifetime in prison. Many whistleblowers charge him with the fact, that he is worse than George W. Bush. Obama also announced that his policy would be less militant. He ended the Iraq War with a troop exit in December 18,

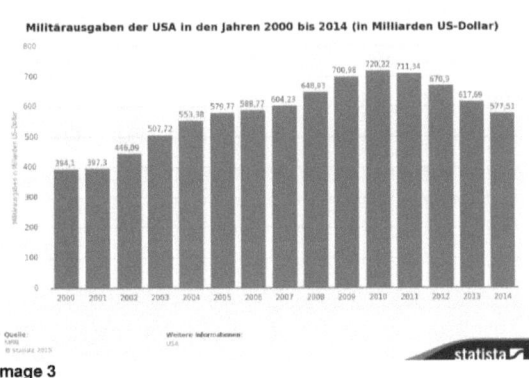
−Image 3

[58] http://www.weitwinkelsubjektiv.com/2014/03/28/der-irak-krieg-und-die-vorherrschaft-des-dollar/ (24.01.2016)
[59] https://en.wikipedia.org/wiki/Iraq_War#Relation_to_the_Global_War_on_Terrorism (09.02.2016)

2011 and he reduced the troops in Afghanistan. In 2017 the war in Afghanistan will be over too he said, although there isn't stabilization at all.[60] He also reduced the military spending after a big increase as we can see in image 4.

He also wants to reform the extremely important weapons law but that won't work, because the lobby is too big and the weapons are too relevant for the Americans.

His ideas of more control over weapon purchases and an obligation for weapon owners is a great attempt but he also knows how important and powerful the weapon industry is, because the USA is still dominating

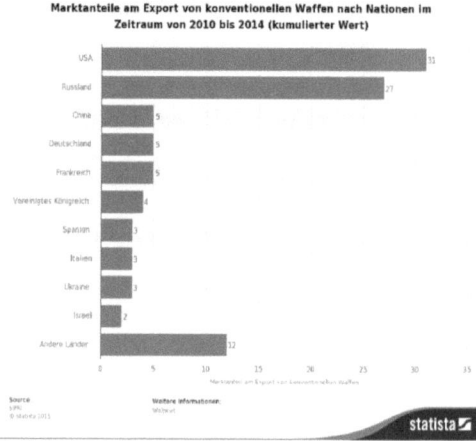

Image 4

the export of weapons, as we can see in image 5.[61]

Quite important too is, that he will expedite and also expedited the offensive and preventive self-defense of the USA against the terrorism.[62] He expanded the espionage more than George W. Bush and he substituted and extended several parts of the Patriot Act. This was not a really good improvement. The killing of Osama bin Laden in May 2, 2011 was a success of his anti-terror policy.

He is also planning to close the prison Guantanamo Bay but the opposition is strict against that. The Congress for example is blocking the financing of the closure because Obama has no explicit plans with the prisoners.[63] Obama just wants end the torture and unlimited imprisonment of the prisoners, which is a good idea.

---

[60] http://www.n-tv.de/politik/dossier/Der-Messias-des-Wandels-article9973411.html (23.01.2016)
[61] http://www.faz.net/aktuell/politik/ausland/amerika/das-waffenrecht-bleibt-auch-mit-obamas-massnahmen-windelweich-13998964.html (24.01.2016)
[62] http://www.uni-heidelberg.de/md/politik/harnisch/person/vortraege/harnisch-us-au_enpolitik_obama_koblenz_2012.pdf (23.01.2016)
[63] http://www.zeit.de/politik/ausland/2015-07/guantanamo-obama-schliessung-kongress-plan (24.01.2016)

All in all we can see that Obama has some good ideas and already implemented some of those, but in some point he has huge enemies and the expansion of the espionage is not good at all.

4.2 Obama and the monitoring by the NSA

Obama announced a more transparency policy regarding the NSA but he is in a twist. His government is stealing data from huge IT- companies but the main sponsors of his election campaign were exactly these companies. He is also spreading anxiety to justify the extension and development of the NSA. He wants to secure that the USA will also be in the future the superpower of the internet In the fight against China. He announced security for Whistleblowers but this only applies for direct employees of the state and not for the private companies. The downplay and alleged unknowing concerning the NSA is also not right, because he is the President and the President determines the focus areas of the espionage. Internal documents are showing that Obama is focusing on terrorism, economical interests, foreign policy and domestic political aims of other states and the financial system and the trade of other states. He also imposed for instance to spy diplomats and embassies like the UN.[64]

5   September 11, 2001 – an inside job?

There are several conspiracy theories and you can find millions of sites and videos on the Internet with information and possible procedures. Most of the conspiracy theories are having two consents: September 11, 2001 has other causes and other delinquents than the US- government is telling us.[65]
The main of the conspiracy theorists are that members of the government have caused, intended the attacks or have let them happen. The reason for this is, in their opinion, that the attacks are planned from people who benefit from such attacks. The USA government needed the agreement for the counterterrorism war and they

---

[64] Der NSA-Kompex, p. 197 et seq.
[65] http://www.zeit.de/2014/45/verschwoerung-11-september-cia (11.02.2016)

wanted to restrict the citizen rights, especially with the Patriot Act. After the attacks everybody agreed and sympathized with the government.

There are two main thoughts: either the government knew from the plans of al-Qaeda and let them happen or the planned and accomplished the attacks themselves to realize their personal interests.[66]

Several grotesque theories are trying to explain the attacks, for instance:

- The government demolished the World Trade Center and there were no airplanes.
- The airplanes were full of bombs and they were controlled remotely.
- The Jews or Israel are responsible for the attacks or they knew it before it happened. (Quite unrealistic)
- The government faked the video of Osama bin Laden explaining that the attacks were planned from al-Qaeda to distract the media from themselves.

The theorists have a lot of evidences to proof their theories, for example:

- The statement of an ex-pilot of a CIA agent under oath who says, that there weren't any airplanes.[67]
- The scaffold of the WTC should have withstood such a crash.[68]
- The president George W. Bush said that he has seen the first attack on TV and thought that it was an accident, but no one broadcasted this attack.

Most of these theories are quite grotesque and unrealistic, but we should review the official explanations critically.

---

[66] https://en.wikipedia.org/wiki/9/11_conspiracy_theories (11.02.2016)
[67] http://www.pravda-tv.com/2014/06/911-ex-cia-pilot-sagt-unter-eid-aus-das-die-zwillingsturme-nicht-von-flugzeugen-getroffen-wurden-video/ (10.02.2016)
[68] http://www.n-tv.de/politik/119/Die-vielen-9-11-Luegen-article4268816.html (10.02.2016)

6   Resources

Books:

Rosenbach, Marcel; Stark, Holger: Der NSA-Komplex. Edward Snowden und der Weg in die totale Überwachung, München (Spiegel Buchverlag), 2015.

Wright, Lawrence: Der Tod wird euch finden. Al-Qaida und der Weg zum 11. September, München (Spiegel Buchverlag), 2007.

Keine Macht dem Terror * United we stand. Reden und Ansprachen zum 11. September 2001, Essen (Mundus Media, Ann Arbor), 2001.

Knopp, Guido; Brauburger, Stefan; Arens, Peter: Der heilige Krieg. Mohammed, die Kreuzritter und der 11. September, ;München (C. Bertelsmann), 2011.

Internet resources:

http://communitytable.parade.com/125076/compiledandeditedbysaralukinson/09-tribute-to-9-11/ (21.12.2015)

http://www.history.com/topics/9-11-attacks (21.12.2015)

http://www.tagesspiegel.de/meinung/andere-meinung/gastkommentar-was-9-11-fuer-die-internationale-politik-bedeutet/4593320.html (21.12.2015)

http://www.n-tv.de/politik/119/Der-Verfall-einer-Supermacht-article4260276.html (21.12.2015)

https://www.youtube.com/watch?v=-23kmhc3P8U (21.12.2015)

https://de.wikipedia.org/wiki/Unilateralität (21.12.2015)

https://de.wikipedia.org/wiki/Irakkrieg#Kosten (21.12.2015)

https://www.bpb.de/politik/hintergrund-aktuell/68721/9-11-und-die-folgen-10-09-2012 (21.12.2015)

http://www.dw.com/de/das-sicherheitspolitische-vermächtnis-von-9-11/a-17071606 (21.12.2015)

http://www.dw.com/de/das-sicherheitspolitische-vermächtnis-von-9-11/a-17071606 (21.12.2015) http://www.welt.de/wirtschaft/article119782731/Wie-die-NSA-Verschluesselungen-knackt.html (21.12.2015)

http://www.bayfor.org/media/pdf/zib2_kopp.pdf (21.12.2015)

http://www.n24.de/n24/Wissen/History/d/1343982/reaktionen-aus-aller-welt.html (03.01.2016)

http://www.history.com/topics/reaction-to-9-11 (03.01.2016)

http://www.bpb.de/politik/extremismus/islamismus/36374/al-qaida (21.01.2016) and (08.02.2016)

http://news.bbc.co.uk/2/shared/spl/hi/pop_ups/04/world_al_qaeda/html/2.stm (21.01.2016)

http://www.infoplease.com/spot/al-qaeda-terrorism.html (21.01.2016)

http://www.sueddeutsche.de/politik/westliche-geiseln-eu-laender-finanzieren-al-qaida-mit-millionen-loesegeldern-1.2069656 (21.01.2016)

http://www.wiwo.de/politik/ausland/al-qaida-dem-geld-der-terroristen-auf-der-spur-seite-3/4637972-3.html (21.01.2016)

http://www.spiegel.de/politik/ausland/saudi-arabien-al-qaida-angeblich-vom-koenigshaus-finanziert-a-1016612.html (21.01.2016)

http://www.terrorismanalysts.com/pt/index.php/pot/article/view/113/html (23.01.2016)

http://www.n-tv.de/politik/dossier/Der-Messias-des-Wandels-article9973411.html (23.01.2016)

http://www.uni-heidelberg.de/md/politik/harnisch/person/vortraege/harnisch-us-au__enpolitik_obama_koblenz__2012.pdf (23.01.2016)

http://www.zeit.de/politik/ausland/2015-07/guantanamo-obama-schliessung-kongress-plan (24.01.2016)

http://www.faz.net/aktuell/politik/ausland/amerika/das-waffenrecht-bleibt-auch-mit-obamas-massnahmen-windelweich-13998964.html (24.01.2016)

http://www.zeit.de/online/2008/09/stiglitz-irakkrieg-kosten/komplettansicht (24.01.2016)

http://www.zeit.de/politik/ausland/2010-02/patriot-act-zweifel (24.01.2016)

http://www.weitwinkelsubjektiv.com/2014/03/28/der-irak-krieg-und-die-vorherrschaft-des-dollar/ (24.01.2016)

http://www.breitbart.com/national-security/2015/05/19/5-reasons-the-iraq-war-was-not-a-mistake/ (24.01.2016)

http://www.zeit.de/2013/12/Irakkrieg-Folgen-Bilanz (24.01.2016) https://www.lpb-bw.de/irak_krieg.html (24.01.2016)

https://en.wikipedia.org/wiki/Iraq_War (24.01.2016)

http://www.e-ir.info/2015/03/09/one-war-many-reasons-the-us-invasion-of-iraq/ (24.01.2016)

http://www.nationalreview.com/article/343870/why-did-we-invade-iraq-victor-davis-hanson (24.01.2016)

http://www.theatlantic.com/politics/archive/2015/05/the-right-and-wrong-questions-about-the-iraq-war/393497/ (24.01.2016)

https://www.opensocietyfoundations.org/events/usa-patriot-acts-effect-civil-liberties (07.02.2016)

http://www.taz.de/!5080880/ (07.02.2016)

http://searchdatamanagement.techtarget.com/definition/Patriot-Act (07.02.2016)

http://www.dw.com/de/usa-patriot-act-das-neue-anti-terror-paket/a-351266 (07.02.2016)

http://pretioso-blog.com/was-man-ueber-den-usa-patriot-act-wissen-sollte/#.VrdltcdK1uU (07.02.2016)

http://www.faz.net/aktuell/politik/ausland/antiterrorgesetze-patriot-act-gilt-weiter-1637729.html (07.02.2016)

http://communitytable.parade.com/125076/compiledandeditedbysaralukinson/09-tribute-to-9-11/ (07.02.2016)

https://en.wikipedia.org/wiki/Mohammed_bin_Awad_bin_Laden#Wives_and_children (08.02.2016)

http://www.infoplease.com/spot/al-qaeda-terrorism.html (08.02.2016)

https://en.wikipedia.org/wiki/Al-Qaeda (08.02.2016)

https://en.wikipedia.org/wiki/September_11_attacks#Planning_of_the_attacks (08.02.2016)

http://voices.nationalgeographic.com/2011/09/07/the-original-plans-for-911/ (08.02.2016)

http://www.zeit.de/politik/2015-06/us-senat-patriot-acts (09.02.2016)

https://www.rt.com/usa/264005-freedom-patriot-act-surveillance/ (09.02.2016)

https://en.wikipedia.org/wiki/Iraq_War#Relation_to_the_Global_War_on_Terrorism (09.02.2016)

https://en.wikipedia.org/wiki/Foreign_Intelligence_Surveillance_Act (10.02.2016)

https://en.wikipedia.org/wiki/Booz_Allen_Hamilton (10.02.2016) http://www.handelsblatt.com/technik/it-internet/rechenzentrum-des-geheimdiensts-nsa-platz-fuer-fuenf-billionen-gigabyte/8315424.html (10.02.2016)

http://www.theatlantic.com/technology/archive/2015/11/a-visit-to-the-nsas-data-center-in-utah/416691/ (10.02.2016)

http://www.zeit.de/2014/45/verschwoerung-11-september-cia (11.02.2016)

https://en.wikipedia.org/wiki/9/11_conspiracy_theories (11.02.2016)

http://www.pravda-tv.com/2014/06/911-ex-cia-pilot-sagt-unter-eid-aus-das-die-zwillingsturme-nicht-von-flugzeugen-getroffen-wurden-video/ (10.02.2016)

http://www.n-tv.de/politik/119/Die-vielen-9-11-Luegen-article4268816.html (10.02.2016)

Images:

Image 1 (not in publication):

http://eyesopenreport.com/wp-content/uploads/2015/07/11_9.jpg (10.02.2016)

Image 2:

https://upload.wikimedia.org/wikipedia/commons/f/fe/Flight_paths_of_hijacked_planes-September_11_attacks.jpg (09.02.2016)

Image 3:

https://upload.wikimedia.org/wikipedia/commons/thumb/5/5f/UKUSA_Map.svg/940px-UKUSA_Map.svg.png (10.02.2016)

Image 4:

http://de.statista.com/statistik/daten/studie/183059/umfrage/militaerausgaben-der-usa/ (24.01.2016)

Image 5:

http://de.statista.com/statistik/daten/studie/151877/umfrage/weltweite-marktanteile-am-export-von-konventionellen-waffen-nach-nationen/ (24.01.2016)